EXTENDING SCIENCE 2

WATER
Selected Topics

Extending Science Series

EXTENDING SCIENCE

SCIENCE

2

WATER

Selected Topics

E N Ramsden BSc PhD DPhil
R E Lee BSc

Stanley Thornes (Publishers) Ltd

First published 1983 by
Stanley Thornes (Publishers) Ltd,
Educa House,
Old Station Drive,
Leckhampton Road,
CHELTENHAM GL53 0DN

British Library Cataloguing in Publication Data
Ramsden, E N
 Water.—(Extending science; 2)
 1. Water.—Juvenile literature
 I. Title   II. Lee, R E   III. Series
 553.7   TD348
 ISBN 0-85950-389-5

Typeset by Quadraset Ltd, Radstock, Bath, Avon
Printed and bound in Great Britain by Bell and Bain Ltd, Thornliebank, Glasgow

CONTENTS

Chapter 1 We Need Water

Chapter 2 Water for Agriculture

Chapter 3 Water for Washing

Chapter 4   **The Boundless Sea**

PREFACE

We have written this book because the subject of water and the pollution of water interests us. It is not intended to provide the complete coverage of water that is required for an examination course: information and experiments which can be found readily in textbooks have not been included. Our hope is that children will find the topics we have covered interesting and see the importance of conserving our environment. We offer this book to teachers to use in any manner which suits them and their pupils. It may be used as extension material in a junior chemistry course or as part of a general science course. It may be used as background material for older pupils who are following an examination course in science or environmental studies. We hope that older pupils who find a traditional course too academic for their liking may find some interesting reading here.

E N Ramsden
Wolfreton School, Hull
R E Lee
St George's College, Weybridge

ACKNOWLEDGEMENTS

We are grateful to Mr J R Dennison and Mr B Rogers, who read the original draft and made many helpful suggestions. Miss Laura Hale has given invaluable assistance with the diagrams, and Mr D F Manley of ST(P) has made significant improvements in the crosswords and supplied the wordfinder. We thank our publishers for the enthusiasm and attention to detail which have gone into the production of this book, and our families for their encouragement.

The authors and publishers are grateful to the following who provided photographs and gave permission for reproduction:

Barnaby's Picture Library (p. 23); The British Oxygen Company Ltd (p. 33); Esso Petroleum Company Ltd (p. 46); Donald Innes (p. 6 centre, bottom, p. 10 top); Mansell Collection (pp. 2, 5); Northumbrian Water Authority (p. 3); Popperfoto (p. 22, p. 45 top); Robert Roskrow Photography (p. 45 bottom); Ian Ross (p. 8); Syndication International (p. 47); Thames Water Authority (p. 7); Wessex Water Authority (p. 10 centre); Yorkshire Water Authority (p. 6 top).

CHAPTER 1

WE NEED WATER

CAN YOU IMAGINE LIFE WITHOUT RUNNING WATER?

We use plenty of water. The sketches below show some ways in which we use water. No doubt you will be able to think of many more.

What use is water?

1

We use more water for washing than people did a century ago. We use 50 litres (10 gallons) a day for flushing the toilet. Our homes, schools and factories need a plentiful supply of water. Where does it all come from? The water we use comes from rivers and lakes to reservoirs for storage. From these, it goes to water-works to be made fit to be piped into our homes. Used water passes from our buildings to sewer pipes. These lead to a sewage-works. Here, waste water is purified and returned to a river. To appreciate what the water-works and sewage-works do for us, we need to look into the history books.

In the nineteenth century, only rich people had water laid on to their houses. Poorer people often collected rain-water in tubs beside their houses. The rain had fallen through smoke and grime, and collected more dirt while in the tub. Some people had wells and pumped water from them up to street level. The well-water could be fouled by water seeping into it from a nearby cesspit. (A cesspit was what the toilets emptied into.)

Most of the water for town dwellers came from water companies. In London, some of these took water from the River Thames and pumped it without any treatment along the mains into their streets or houses. Since the sewers emptied into the Thames, the companies were selling diluted sewage as drinking water! This led to disease. The dreadful diseases of cholera, typhoid, tuberculosis and smallpox were common.

A stand-pipe in 1860

The water was supplied to a stand-pipe in the street for a few hours a day. There were so many houses to each stand-pipe that a crowd of people would rush to get water when the supply was turned on. Often, they had no time to collect enough for their needs. They could not hope to keep clean. They had insufficient water to wash their clothes or themselves, and they smelled horrible.

Outside London, there were some better water companies. Some filtered water through beds of sand and gravel before pumping it to the people.

Things are very different now. A modern water-works is very careful to make the water fit to drink.

DRINKING-WATER FROM RIVER-WATER

Water is taken from rivers and reservoirs in tunnels to the treatment works. There it is made fit to drink. The photograph below shows the Kielder Reservoir and Dam in Northumbria, which were opened in 1982. Seven miles long and half a mile wide, the reservoir is the largest man-made lake in Europe. The reservoir holds 200 billion litres of water, and supplies 1000 million litres a day to the homes and industries of north-eastern England. The surrounding countryside is being developed as a recreation area.

Kielder Reservoir and Dam

The next illustration shows the treatment which reservoir-water receives. Rubbish is removed, solid material is allowed to settle, and the water is filtered. Chlorine is added to kill germs, and the water is fit to drink.

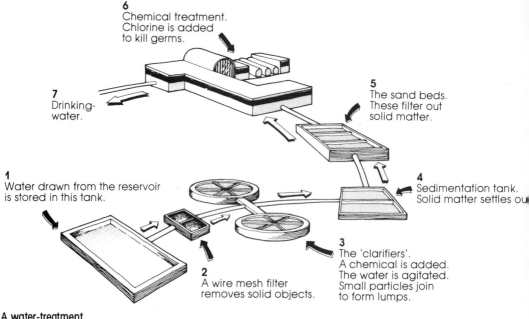

6
Chemical treatment.
Chlorine is added
to kill germs.

7
Drinking-
water.

5
The sand beds.
These filter out
solid matter.

1
Water drawn from the reservoir
is stored in this tank.

4
Sedimentation tank.
Solid matter settles ou

3
The 'clarifiers'.
A chemical is added.
The water is agitated.
Small particles join
to form lumps.

2
A wire mesh filter
removes solid objects.

A water-treatment
works

Some of the water we use comes from underground sources.
This water does not need the complete treatment. It is simply
pumped out of the ground and chlorinated.

CASE HISTORY (1)

The River Thames: Will the salmon return now the sewage has gone?

The Thames rises in high ground and flows to the sea. Over
the 70 mile stretch from Teddington to the North Sea, the
Thames is tidal. It ebbs and flows with the North Sea. For this
reason, any pollutants in the Thames are not washed out to sea
but float to and fro with the tide. As pollution increases, the
number of fish that can live in the river decreases. Until about
1750, there were salmon in the Thames. They need plenty of
dissolved oxygen in the water. From 1750 onwards, pollution
became more and more severe, and the level of dissolved oxygen fell. The reason for this was the expansion of London.

More and more people were living in London, and there was
more and more human waste to dispose of. Only wealthy people
had a lavatory in the house. The poor had a 'privy' shared
between several houses. The privy was a shed with a wooden
seat inside, below which was a cesspit. When the cesspit was
full, it had to be emptied by workmen. They wheeled the unpleasant contents of the cesspit away in carts. The people who
did this job were called 'nightmen'. Why do you think they
were made to do this job at night?

People with houses on the river banks built privies overhanging the water so that they would empty straight into the river. If you look at the drawing below, you will see the privies alongside the river.

Underground sewers had been built since 1550, to carry away rain-water. They were not originally intended to take away refuse. When the water-closet was invented, the contents of the toilet were washed by a stream of water into a cesspit outside the house. As the problem of emptying the cesspits grew, the toilets were discharged into drains running into street sewers, and then, without any treatment, into the Thames. Bacteria in the river broke down the sewage in the water into harmless substances.

Old houses in London Street, Dockhead, about 1810

The Metropolitan Commissioners of Sewers were founded in 1843. They liked the mysterious way in which the river disposed of their sewage. (Bacteria are still a mystery to some people!) They did away with 200 000 smelly cesspits. Water-closets took over, and their contents were drained into the river. Bacteria multiplied, feeding on this sewage. Much of the oxygen in the water was used up by the bacteria. Some bacteria became short of oxygen, and died. The remaining bacteria could not cope with all the sewage, and the sewage content of the river increased. It was carried to and fro on the tide. When it reached Westminster, the Members of Parliament found the stench unbearable. They debated methods of dealing with the nuisance, but could not agree on a course of action. Meanwhile, germs were breeding in the sewage.

5

(a)

(a) Aeration tanks, (b) and (c) filter beds in a modern sewage-works

(b)

(c)

The Thames water was used as drinking-water. Such foul water was the cause of several epidemics. Epidemics of cholera broke out in 1831, killing 7000 people, and in 1848, killing 15 000 people. Parliament decided to try to get rid of the sewage.

The Metropolitan Board of Works was founded in 1855. The Board had the sewage carried in large sewers down to two reservoirs 30 miles downstream of London Bridge. These large reservoirs held the sewage and released it when the tide went out. The hope was that the river would carry all the sewage out to sea. The huge volume of sewage was too much, however, and the river could not cope with it.

In 1880, they began to treat sewage with lime. The treatment was carried out in covered channels. The solids which settled to the bottom of the channels were carried out to sea in ships and dumped. The liquid from the channels was discharged into the river. The population continued to expand, and the river continued to be foul. Around 1890, a man called Dibden had the brilliant idea of arranging for living organisms to feed on the sewage. He allowed sewage to trickle through towers filled with coke. The coke contained plenty of air, and bacteria grew in the towers and fed on the sewage. Dibden had invented the biological filter method of purification which is still in use today. The photographs opposite show aeration tanks and filter beds in a modern sewage-works.

In 1930, a huge new sewage-works for the whole of London was built at Mogden. Bacteria were used to break down the sewage to harmless products. In 1964, the big plant at Crossness opened, and started to treat 500 million litres of sewage a day. Beckton sewage-works opened 10 years later. The photograph below shows a scene in the laboratories of Beckton Works. Samples are taken and analysed at all stages of treatment.

Laboratory in Beckton sewage-works

The improvement in the Thames was spectacular. The graph below shows how the level of dissolved oxygen shot up after 1964.

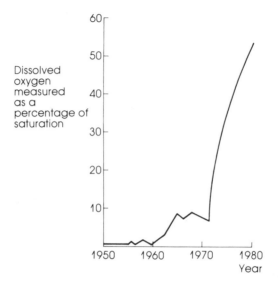

The level of dissolved oxygen in the Thames

Fish started to return from the sea to the river. Plaice, herring, sole and 40 other kinds of fish are now found in the Thames. Formerly, only the eel, which can survive in foul water, was found. Will the salmon ever return to the Thames? To find out, scientists have put marked salmon into the river. They swim downstream to the sea. If they return, they will be identified by their markings. Then we shall know that the Thames is clean again. It would be a fitting end to the success story of the Thames! The photograph below shows someone enjoying their leisure on the Thames (he fell off immediately the photograph was taken!).

Recreation on the Thames

HOW WATER IS TREATED IN A MODERN SEWAGE-WORKS

A sewage-works prepares water for returning to a river. The stages of treatment are shown in the diagram below.

The water discharged into the river looks clear. It contains a little suspended matter, some dissolved chemicals and some germs. Bacteria in the river purify the water. There must be enough oxygen dissolved in the water to keep the bacteria alive. If the river becomes too poor in oxygen, the bacteria die, and the sewage content of the water increases.

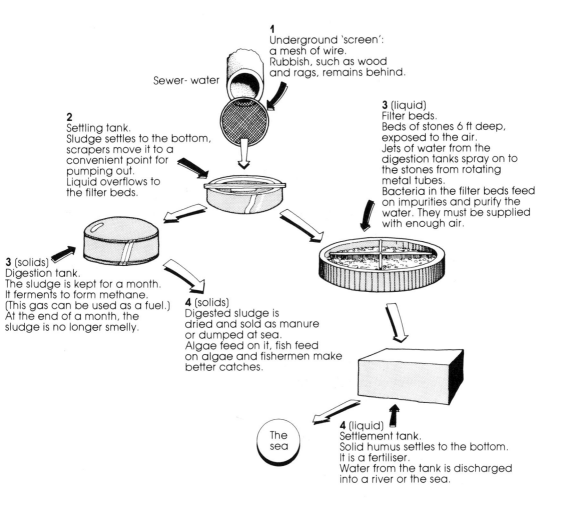

1
Underground 'screen':
a mesh of wire.
Rubbish, such as wood
and rags, remains behind.

Sewer- water

2
Settling tank.
Sludge settles to the bottom,
scrapers move it to a
convenient point for
pumping out.
Liquid overflows to
the filter beds.

3 (liquid)
Filter beds.
Beds of stones 6 ft deep,
exposed to the air.
Jets of water from the
digestion tanks spray on to
the stones from rotating
metal tubes.
Bacteria in the filter beds feed
on impurities and purify the
water. They must be supplied
with enough air.

3 (solids)
Digestion tank.
The sludge is kept for a month.
It ferments to form methane.
(This gas can be used as a fuel.)
At the end of a month, the
sludge is no longer smelly.

4 (solids)
Digested sludge is
dried and sold as manure
or dumped at sea.
Algae feed on it, fish feed
on algae and fishermen make
better catches.

The
sea

4 (liquid)
Settlement tank.
Solid humus settles to the bottom.
It is a fertiliser.
Water from the tank is discharged
into a river or the sea.

The sewage-works

The photographs on the next page show the sedimentation tanks (or settling tanks) at a sewage-works, and a sludge ship, used to carry sludge out to sea for dumping.

Sedimentation tanks

Sludge ship

Not all sewage is treated at sewage-works. Untreated sewage is still discharged into rivers and the sea. Sewage is made up of compounds which contain carbon, hydrogen and oxygen, some nitrogen and some sulphur. All of these are oxidised by oxygen to harmless compounds. None of these oxidation products is unpleasant or smelly. If too much sewage is present in water, all the oxygen is used up. The sewage is then attacked by different bacteria, which do not need oxygen. They turn sewage into methane, CH_4, and the smelly gases, ammonia, NH_3 (the 'nappies' smell), and hydrogen sulphide, H_2S (the 'bad eggs' smell). Thus, in the absence of oxygen, unpleasant decay products are formed. The presence of dissolved oxygen in the water is all-important.

THE WATER CYCLE

Nature provides us with fresh water. Rain-water seeps through the ground and collects in streams, rivers and lakes for us to use. Trees draw in water through their roots. After they have extracted the useful salts from the water, they pass water vapour out of their leaves. This process is called *transpiration*. Animals drink water from streams and rivers. The water they excrete passes back to the soil, and the water vapour they breathe out puts water back into circulation.

The warmth of the sun causes evaporation of water from rivers, lakes and seas. Water vapour passes upwards, until it reaches cooler air and condenses to form clouds of tiny droplets of water. When the clouds are cooled, they release water as rain. This cycle of events is called the *water cycle*.

The diagram below shows how we modify the water cycle. Water is taken from the river to a water-treatment works. From here, it is supplied to houses and factories. After use, it goes to the sewage-works. After treatment at the sewage-works, it is pure enough to be discharged into the sea.

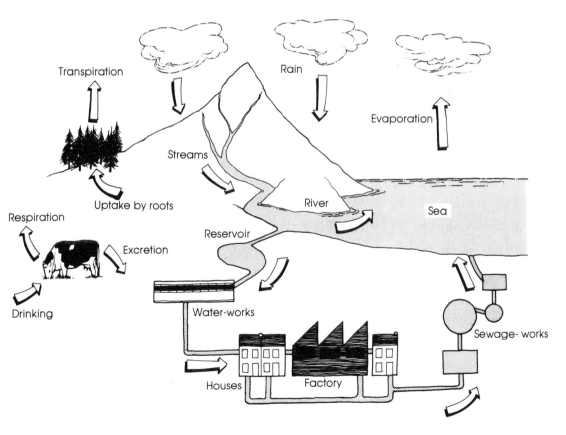

The water cycle

Does this water look polluted?

Not every country can take safe water for granted as we can in the United Kingdom. In many poor countries, children are dying through drinking infected water. In some countries, the drinking water is polluted by sewage as it was in the United Kingdom 200 years ago. The World Health Organization has figures to show that 80 per cent of all the disease in the world is linked with water. The United Nations has set itself a target date of 1990. By that year, the UN aims to have safe water and sanitation in every country.

Water contains dissolved air. This is very important as it allows fish and other water animals to breathe. Air is more soluble in cold water than in hot water. If water is warmed up, dissolved air will come out of solution. If a river becomes too warm, fish find they have less dissolved oxygen to breathe. Some industries need water for cooling purposes. They take water from a river, use it to cool their plant, and return it to the river. A plant which uses a great deal of water for cooling is a nuclear power plant. This can warm up a river by several degrees. It results in less air being available for fish. This problem has not occurred in the United Kingdom. It is more likely to happen in warmer climates. It is called *thermal pollution*, and is most serious when it occurs in rivers which are already short of oxygen on account of some other form of pollution.

THE OXYGEN NEEDS OF SOME ANIMALS

If waste materials are put into a stream or river, they damage the plant and animal life in the water. The water is said to be *polluted*. Some factories discharge waste into rivers. Sewage is another pollutant which is discharged into rivers. Sewage decays gradually to form harmless substances. Dissolved oxygen is used in the decay process. If there is not enough oxygen in the water, decay cannot take place. Sewage then accumulates, and the water becomes foul.

To find out whether the water in a river is rich or poor in oxygen, you can look at the animals in the river. The diagram below shows some aquatic (water-dwelling) animals. The rat-tailed maggot can survive in water containing very little dissolved oxygen because it breathes air from the surface of the water through a long air tube. The little red sludgeworm can also survive in polluted water as it feeds on decaying plants. If these are the only animals you can find, you know the water is highly polluted. The bright-red bloodworm and the water louse can survive in fairly polluted water as they feed on decaying plants. If the grey freshwater shrimp and the caddis fly larva are found, then you know that the degree of pollution is slight. These animals need more oxygen than the worms and need fresh plants to feed on. If you can see the stonefly larva and the mayfly larva, then you know the water is clean, because these animals cannot live in polluted water.

Some aquatic animals

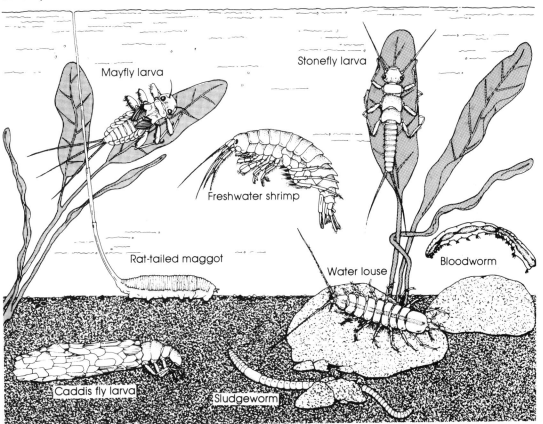

Mayfly larva

Stonefly larva

Freshwater shrimp

Rat-tailed maggot

Water louse

Bloodworm

Caddis fly larva

Sludgeworm

The River Irwell

The Irwell rises in the Pennine Hills. It wends its way down to Manchester, where it joins the Manchester Ship Canal. This flows into the Mersey Estuary and out to the Irish Sea. A stretch of the Irwell is shown in the diagram below. It takes waste material from all these factories. Little wonder that in 1970 it was the most polluted river in England! Since 1970, the industries on its banks have controlled the amount of waste they discharge into it. The level of dissolved oxygen has risen, and fish and plants live in the water again.

The River Irwell

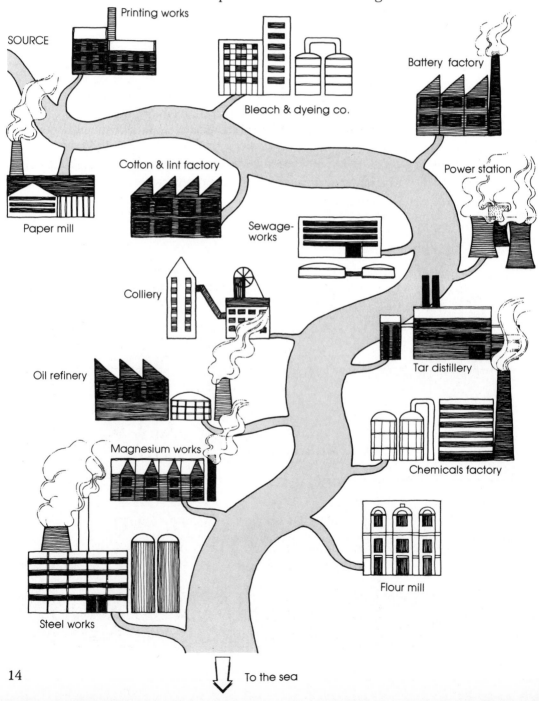

SOURCE

Printing works

Battery factory

Bleach & dyeing co.

Cotton & lint factory

Power station

Paper mill

Sewage-works

Colliery

Tar distillery

Oil refinery

Magnesium works

Chemicals factory

Flour mill

Steel works

14 ⬇ To the sea

WORDFINDER ON SEWAGE

Copy out (or photocopy) the grid below and then see if you can find answers to the 26 clues. One has been ringed and you can ring the other 25. Three of the answers each consist of two words.

The words read from right to left or from left to right horizontally and from top to bottom or from bottom to top vertically. Do not write on this page.

1 London river (6)
2 It swam in 1 until about 1750 (6)
3 The level of dissolved ____ in 1 went up after 1964 (6)
4 It goes over 1 (6, 6)
5 They emptied cesspits (8)
6 This disease killed 15 000 people in London in 1848 (7)
7 They can break down sewage (8)
8 He invented a way of dealing with sewage (6)
9 They need very little 3 (4)
10 A gas that smells of nappies (7)
11 A sewage-works for London was built at ____ in 1930 (6) . . .
12 . . . and another one at ____ in 1964 (9) . . .
13 . . . ____ sewage-works opened 10 years later (7)
14 In 1970 it was the most polluted river in England (7)

15 Part of a modern sewage-works (8, 4) . . .
16 . . . where ____ goes to the bottom (6)
17 A gas from sewage with the formula CH_4 (7)
18 Water is purified in the ____ beds of a sewage-works (6)
19, 20 A gas that smells of bad eggs (8, 8: two words in different places)
21, 22 If a river warms up by several degrees there is less ____ available for ____ (3, 4: two words in different places)
23 In the formula NH_3, N stands for ____ (8)
24 In the formula CH_4, C stands for ____ (6)
25 At one time sewage was carried out to ____ and dumped (3)
26 An essential part of the water cycle (4)

```
T H A M E S N E G O R D Y H
C S L C A R B O N S D W N A
B I B A C T E R I A I L I K
A F O S L U D G E L B O G N
I C M F I L T E R M D N H A
N L O T N E G Y X O E D T T
O T G I R W E L L N N O M G
M X D B D E M E T H A N E N
M B E C K T O N W S M B N I
A A N N N U P S N I A R M L
D E I A C H O L E R A I S T
G S L I Z S U L P H I D E T
N I T R O G E N M P O G A E
S L E E D C R O S S N E S S
```

15

Study the animal life in a river

An interesting activity is to carry out a study of a river in your area. The animals you find (see page 13) will tell you how clear or polluted the water is. You will need a net and a magnifying glass and instructions from your teacher or from a book such as *The Pollution Handbook* by Richard Mabey (Penguin Education, 1974).

How much water do you use?

Have you any idea how much water you use in a day? We suggest you tackle this activity at home.

1) Find out how much water is needed for each of the following uses:
   (a) filling a kettle
   (b) filling a watering can
   (c) cooking a meal
   (d) half-filling a bath
   (e) filling a sink with enough water for washing-up.
Check your answers against those on page 54. These are given in litres and gallons; 1 gallon (8 pints) is 4.5 litres.

16

2) Say how much water you think the average person uses each day for:
   (a) cooking and drinking
   (b) washing and bathing
   (c) laundry
   (d) flushing the lavatory
   (e) gardening
   (f) dishwashing.

Compare your answers with those on page 54. The Water Boards tell us that each person uses about 140 litres (31 gallons) a day.

3) Have you a tap that drips? Put a measuring jug under the tap. Find out how much water comes from the tap in 10 minutes. Calculate how much water comes from the tap in 24 hours.

   The Water Boards reckon that waste from dripping taps takes 20 litres (4.4 gallons) a day of the 140 litres (31 gallons) we use.

Questions for discussion

We suggest that you may like to tackle this work in small groups. Then you can pool ideas.

1) Some people suggest that it would be a good idea to have water-meters in houses. These would measure the amount of water that house used. Then the family would be charged for the water they had used. The idea is to make people more careful in their use of water. Do you think it is a good idea? Would it be a fair scheme? Can you see any disadvantages?

2) Imagine that very little rain falls this summer. Your town is running short of water. If you were in charge, what restrictions would you make on the use of water to make the supply last as long as possible?

3) Make a list of all the things you use water for in your home.

4) Make a list of the industries in your nearest town. How many of them are big users of water?

5) Water is used for recreation. Many sports involve water. Rivers, lakes, reservoirs and the sea are all used for rec-reation. Make a list of water sports. For each sport, say what kind of water is needed and whether the sport will pollute the water.

6) What use can be made of reservoirs for recreation? Bear in mind the need to avoid polluting the water in the reservoir.

7) Think of a lake or a river or a stretch of coastline near you. Describe how you would develop the area for recreation. Make a plan of the area. Describe any roads, buildings, car-parks, etc., that would be needed.

8) Farming is an industry. What type of farming is carried on in your area? Is the rainfall high or low in the area? What type of farming is carried on in areas of (a) high rainfall, (b) low rainfall?

9) Water is used for transport. See what information you can obtain about the importance of rivers and canals for transport. What are the advantages and disadvantages of transporting people and cargoes by water?

10) Water is used for defence. How many examples can you think of in which people have used water as a means of protection?

ACTIVITY 4

Construct a model water-purifier

The diagram below shows one possible model. It is made from a plastics orangeade bottle, from which the bottom has been cut out. The neck is fitted with a rubber bung with a piece of glass tubing through it. The bottle is filled with a layer of large clean stones, then a layer of washed gravel, and finally a layer of washed sand. When muddy water is poured into the top, it should come out of the bottom clean.

A model water-purifier

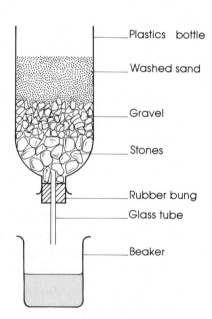

Plastics bottle

Washed sand

Gravel

Stones

Rubber bung

Glass tube

Beaker

Some chemical experiments on water

To do these experiments, you need to obtain water from as many different sources as possible. Examples are:

Rain-water	Water from a stream
Tap-water	Water from a stagnant pond
Sea-water	Water from a river in the countryside
Distilled water	Water from a river in the town

Ask your teacher for practical instructions to help you answer the following questions. The different types of water will give different results. The answers will tell you how pure the different types of water are.

1) How much solid material is present in the water? (Filtration will tell you.)

2) How much dissolved solid is present in the water? (Evaporation will tell you.)

3) Is there dissolved air present in the water? (Warming the water will bring air out of solution.)

4) Is the water acidic or alkaline or neutral? (Universal indicator will tell you.)

QUESTIONS ON WATER TREATMENT

1 Imagine there is a drought, and you and your family have to cut down on water. How could you halve your consumption of water? What is the last thing you would cut down on? What is the first thing you would cut down on?

2 What do people mean when they say that water is 'polluted'? Why is it safe to discharge a small amount of sewage into a river? What is there in the water that is able to break down sewage into harmless products?

3 The term 'water cycle' describes the processes which put water vapour into the air and the processes which take water vapour out of the air. Name two processes which put water vapour into the air. Name two processes which put water into the soil.

4 Where does mains water come from? Where is it stored before treatment? What is done to remove bits of rubbish from the water? How are very small objects removed? What is the name of the living organisms which cannot be removed? What harm is there in letting them remain in the water? What is done about them?

19

5 What is meant by a tidal river? Why is a tidal river likely to become polluted? Name three kinds of pollution that are likely to be discharged into a river.

6 What organisms cause sewage to break down? These organisms multiply if the amount of sewage in the water increases. How does this multiplication lead to their destruction? What do they run short of, and what happens to them? What measures can be taken to prevent the destruction of these organisms?

7 If sewage decays in the absence of oxygen, three gases are formed. One is a flammable gas, which can be used as a fuel. One has a 'nappies' smell, and the third has a 'bad eggs' smell. What are these three gases?

CROSSWORD ON WATER-WORKS AND SEWAGE-WORK

First, trace this grid on to a piece of paper (or photocopy this page). Then fill in the answers. Do not write on this page.

Across

2 Washing-machines put these into the water (4)

4 These small creatures destroy sewage (8)

7 Please _____ when people are talking about pollution (6)

8 The water _____ was much better than the 11 across (6)

9 A home uses _____ gallons of water a day for flushing the toilet (3)

10 They form an entrance for the water you drink (4)

11 An old-fashioned toilet (5)

15 Treat water with this to make it safe to drink (8)

16 People could not do this safely in the Thames 50 years ago (4)

19 Thank you (2)

20 You can store water in this (4)

21 A _____-pipe supplies water (5)

22 The water-closet may be in the smallest _____ (4)

23 Large amounts of water are stored in these (10)

Down

1 This takes waste water away (5)

2 This fish will live only in clean rivers (6)

3 You can do this to get very pure water (6)

4 Opposite of front (4)

5 A dreadful disease spread by foul water (7)

6 When you _____, you lose water through the skin (8)

9 Another dreadful disease spread by foul water (7)

12 This form of water consists of tiny little droplets (4)

13 Water _____ easily from one container to another (5)

14 These are used to take solid matter out of water (7)

17 No one should _____ water (5)

18 You can _____ the surface of water to remove floating objects (4)

CHAPTER 2

WATER FOR AGRICULTURE

CASE HISTORY (3)

Damming the Nile: Has Egypt done the right thing?

'Egypt is the Nile; the Nile is Egypt.' This well-worn saying is a tribute to the importance of the River Nile in the economy of Egypt. Without the Nile flowing through it, Egypt would be a barren desert. Because of the Nile, Egypt has a belt of farmland running alongside each bank of the Nile. Every year, the winter rainfall swells the river. Every year, the Nile used to flood, and the flood waters brought life to the parched land.

The Nile in flood

In 1960, the Egyptian government decided to build a huge dam across the Nile. The idea was to prevent the Nile flooding by holding the water back in a lake called Lake Nasser. The water from the lake could then be channelled to the farmland gradually, instead of all at once. The Dam took 10 years and half a billion pounds to build. It is called the Aswan High Dam, and is one of the greatest engineering achievements in the world. It is more than 2 miles wide, 1000 metres thick at the base and 100 metres high. It was designed by West German engineers, and built with Russian aid.

Lake Nasser is 300 miles long. The waters of Lake Nasser have improved a million acres of land. They guarantee farmers a steady water supply by holding back heavy floods. They provide a reserve for dry years. In 1972, when Africa suffered from drought, Egyptian farmers had the water from Lake Nasser.

The Aswan High Dam

Another benefit which Egypt derives from the Aswan High Dam is electricity. At the Dam, there is an electricity generating station. The pressure of the water behind the Dam is used to drive generators. Half of Egypt's electrical power comes from the Aswan High Dam.

This massive tinkering with Nature has had some side-effects. One serious problem concerns the Nile silt. The Nile contains fine particles of solid, or silt. The silt contains minerals which enrich the soil. All the silt is now trapped behind the Dam. No longer does the Nile carry this fertiliser to the farmlands on its banks. Before the Dam was built, the flood waters of the Nile carried fertile silt to 6 million acres. This vast area now needs artificial fertilisers. Some of these must be imported. A substitute has to be found for the lost silt. No one has yet found a substitute for water!

Another problem is that the sodium chloride (common salt) content of the soil on the banks of the river has increased. In

23

past years, it was washed out by flood waters. Now it builds up. Many crops do not like a high salt content, and yields are low.

There has been another alarming result of building the Dam. The Egyptians suffer from a tropical disease called bilharzia. It is caused by tiny worms attacking the intestines and bladder. It is very unpleasant, causing stomach pains and damage to the liver, lungs and heart. It often shortens the victim's life. There has been a 20 per cent increase in the disease since the Dam was built. The reason is that the disease is carried by a snail which cannot survive in fast-flowing water but thrives in the irrigation canals. The whole of the 330 mile long Lake Nasser is infested with the snail, and it has spread to the canals. A person with the disease can put larvae into the water. The farmworkers work knee deep in the canals, irrigating their fields. They bathe in the canals, do laundry in the canals, and children swim in the canals. The larvae settle on a snail, and hatch into the adult flukes (tiny worms). These can infect any-one wading in the canal. Thus the disease spreads rapidly. It has always been a big problem in Egypt. Half or three-quarters of farm workers have it. There has been a serious increase since the Dam was built. So far, there is no answer to the problem. Victims of the disease can be cured, but if they go back to the fields and start wading in the canal again, they become re-infected.

The life cycle of the bilharzia fluke

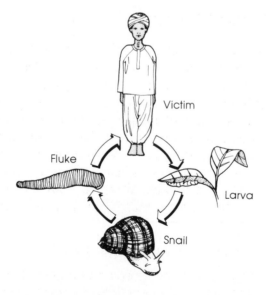

Victim

Fluke

Larva

Snail

Another group of people to suffer from a side-effect of the Dam are the fishermen. The triangular area where the Nile flows into the Mediterranean is called the Delta. It used to be a good fishing ground. Sardines, lobster, shrimp and mackerel were caught there. Preventing the Nile silt from reaching the Delta interferes with the natural food chains. There is little plankton in the water, little for the fish to live on, and so catches are poor.

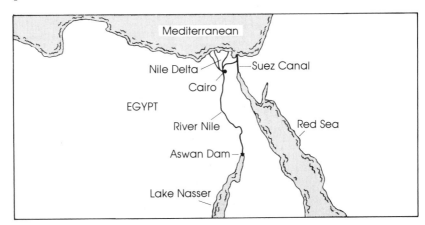

Was the Aswan High Dam a good investment or not? Egypt is still paying for it as she has to repay the loan from Russia. She also has to spend a lot of money on importing fertilisers. Before the Dam was built, the Nile did the job of fertilising for nothing. Lake Nasser is silting up, as the Nile silt builds up behind the Dam. Bilharzia has increased. Was it better to rely on Nature's way—flooding—to water the fields? Can science and technology be used to improve on Nature's way?

PLANTS AND WATER

When you put a plant in water, it takes in water through the roots. Plant cells are *semi-permeable*. This means that they will act as a kind of sieve, allowing water to pass through but stopping dissolved substances from passing. When a concentrated solution and a dilute solution are separated by a semi-permeable *membrane* (a thin piece of tissue, such as a cell wall) water passes from the dilute solution to the more concentrated solution. This process is called *osmosis*. Plant cells contain a dilute solution of salts. When they are placed in water, water passes into the plant cells by the process of osmosis.

ACTIVITY 6

Some experiments on plants and water

We suggest that you design experiments to answer the following questions, and then check out your ideas with your teacher.

Experiment 1
How can you find out (a) the weight of water taken up by the roots of a plant, and (b) the weight of water lost through the leaves by transpiration?

Experiment 2

What happens when you place plant material (such as strips of potato) (a) in water, and (b) in salt solution?

Experiment 3

What happens when a length of visking tubing (a semi-permeable membrane) containing sugar solution is put into a beaker of water?

Experiment 4

What makes pondweed thrive? Take pieces of pondweed in beakers to which you have added water and another substance. You could try manure, compost, fertiliser, detergent, sump oil and many other substances. Control experiments with tap water and distilled water should be done. After 2 or 3 weeks, you will be able to see what has made the pondweed grow best.

ACTIVITY 7

Questions for discussion

This is a complex matter. We suggest that you form groups to discuss these questions. It would help you to get the feel of the arguments if you see what photographs of Egypt you can collect. Look in magazines and geography books. Photographs of the Nile and of farmworkers in the fields would help you.

1) Why did the Egyptian government decide to build the Aswan High Dam?

2) What benefit has the Dam been to farming?

3) Why do farmers now have to buy fertilisers?

4) Lake Nasser is named after a famous Egyptian. Do you know who he was?

5) How long is Lake Nasser?

6) Why is Lake Nasser gradually becoming shallower?

7) If you were a doctor treating a patient for bilharzia, what would you tell him or her to avoid on returning home?

8) If you were working for the Egyptian government, what would you do about the silt accumulating in Lake Nasser? Can you think of a use for the silt?

9) On balance, do you think the Aswan High Dam has been a benefit to Egypt?

10) Suggest what you would do to cure the problems it has created.

QUESTIONS ON WATER AND AGRICULTURE

1   Supply words to fill the blanks in this passage. Do not write on this page.

Plants need water. They take in water through the ＿＿＿ by the process of ＿＿＿. This process occurs when a ＿＿＿ solution is separated from a dilute solution by a ＿＿＿ membrane. Water passes ＿＿＿ the ＿＿＿ solution ＿＿＿ the dilute solution. Plants give out water through the ＿＿＿ by the process of ＿＿＿.

2   What has to be done to make plant cells take in water? What has to be done to make plant cells lose water? Describe an experiment which will demonstrate both of these happenings.

3   Crops need water. What do farmers do in countries with low rainfall to bring water to their crops? How did the farmers on the banks of the Nile water their fields 20 years ago, and how do they do it now? Which method do you think is better? Explain your answer.

4   Bilharzia is a disease which occurs among Egyptian farm workers. Why has it become more common? What can a farm worker do to avoid catching the disease?

CROSSWORD ON WATER AND AGRICULTURE

First, trace this grid on to a piece of paper (or photocopy this page). Then fill in the answers. Do not write on this page.

Across

1 Floating objects _____ with the tide (5)
3 They hatch into flukes (6)
6 Has any answer been found to 21 across? (2)
7 This is how plants take in water (7)
9 It was built across 6 down (3)
11 The triangular region of 6 down (5)
14 See 4 down (3)
15 You often get this with 1 down (4)
16 A town with supposedly health-giving water (3)
18 Not me! (3)
19 Fine particles of solid in 6 down (4)
21 Most Egyptian farm workers have this disease (9)
22 We all _____ water (4)

Down

1 This is what you get without rain or floods (7)

2 The Egyptians wanted more of this when they built 10 across (4)
3 19 across was _____ to the farmers when the 9 across was built (4)
4, 14 across   Water to the east of Egypt (3, 3)
5 Egypt's _____ was to prevent 6 down flooding (3)
6 Egypt's most important river (4)
8 South-east (2)
10 Donkey hidden by Nasser! (3)
12 The _____ content of the soils on the banks of 6 down has increased (4)
13 Where not to swim if you want to avoid 22 across (5)
16 The famous 13 down connecting 4 down, 14 across to the Mediterranean (4)
17 The name of Egypt's famous 9 across (5)
18 In a dry _____ 20 down Nasser provides a reserve of water (4)
20 Nasser is one in Egypt (4)

CHAPTER 3

WATER FOR WASHING

WHAT IS SOAP? HOW DOES IT WORK?

If dust falls on to clothes, it can be brushed off. If oil or grease get on to clothes, they are difficult to remove. Dust sticks to the grease, and the clothes become dirty. The problem in washing clothes is to remove oil and grease. Soaps and detergents can both do this.

A soap consists of sodium ions and soap ions. An ion is an atom or group of atoms which carries an electrical charge. A sodium ion has a positive charge, and a soap ion has a negative charge. (This should, to give it its proper name, be called a hexadecanoate ion, but we are going to call it a *soap ion*.) Each soap ion consists of two parts, a 'head' and a 'tail'. The head is water-loving, and the tail hates water but is attracted to oil and grease.

This chain of $-CH_2-$ groups is the water-hating 'tail'

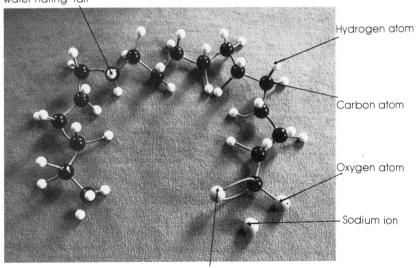

Hydrogen atom

Carbon atom

Oxygen atom

Sodium ion

This $-CO_2^-$ group is the water-loving 'head'

A model of the soap, sodium hexadecanoate

29

In the next diagram, the soap ion is drawn as:

HEAD
Water-loving

TAIL
Water-hating; attracted to grease

The diagram below shows how soap ions dislodge grease from cloth. The head of each ion is attracted to the water. The tail is attracted to a grease particle. As a blob of grease becomes surrounded by soap ions, the soap ions form a bridge between the grease and the water. When they are washed, by hand or in a washing-machine, clothes are swirled around. This action dislodges the blob of grease surrounded by soap ions from the cloth, and it floats off into the water. The dirty water must be removed by rinsing. However good the soap is, if rinsing is not thorough, dirt and grease will go back on to the cloth.

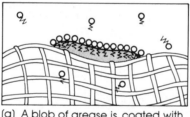

(a) A blob of grease is coated with water-hating tails of soap ions

(b) The blob of grease is squeezed away from the fibre so that the water-loving heads can be surrounded by water

The action of soap on grease

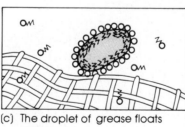

(c) The droplet of grease floats away

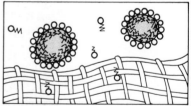

(d) Droplets of grease are prevented from touching by their coating of water-loving heads; they remain spread out through the water

Soaps are made from fats and oils. The process is called *saponification*. The fat or oil must be boiled with a strong alkali. Then salt is added to help the soap to separate out from solution.

DETERGENTS

Detergents are similar to soaps. They also have a chain of —CH_2— groups, which form a water-hating tail. The difference is in the water-loving head. It is a group which contains sulphur and has the formula —SO_3^-. Soaps and detergents are affected differently by hard water.

HARD AND SOFT WATER

We say that water is 'hard' if it is hard to obtain a lather with soap. Detergents will still lather in hard water.

Hard water (on the right), and soft water (on the left) lathering with soap

Why does hard water stop soap from lathering? The reason is that hard water contains calcium and magnesium compounds. The ions of these metals can combine with soap, and, when they do, they form insoluble compounds. We call these insoluble compounds *scum*. You have seen scum floating on top of water. Scum is not formed by detergents. You know that, if you do go on adding soap, you will eventually get a lather. This happens when there are no more calcium and magnesium ions left to form scum.

'Softening' water means removing calcium and magnesium ions. Then, soap will lather instead of forming a scum (see Activity 8).

31

Lake Erie: A matter of death and life

In Canada, there is a string of enormous lakes called the Great Lakes. The map below shows where they are. Lake Ontario and Lake Erie form the border between Canada and the United States. The famous Niagara Falls lie between Lake Ontario and Lake Erie. They are one of the most beautiful sights in the world. No one could imagine, looking at them, that it would be possible to pollute such a vast quantity of water.

The Great Lakes

Lake Erie measures 250 miles by 60 miles. People like sailing on it because they can very soon get out of sight of land and enjoy a wonderful feeling of being 'away from it all'. It is not as vast as the sea, but it is much calmer for sailing. It is such a large lake that no one thought it would hurt to discharge a little sewage and factory waste into it.

They had not reckoned with the algae. Algae are the small green plant life that you see floating on small ponds. No one imagined they could take over one of the Great Lakes. Sewage entering the Lake contains nitrogen compounds, and algae feed on nitrogen compounds. Fertilisers washing into the Lake from the surrounding farms nourish the algae. Detergents are discharged into the Lake. They contain phosphates, on which algae thrive. The algae fed on all these waste materials being washed into the Lake. They formed a thick, green slime. Swimmers found themselves trailing ribbons of green slime. Boating became difficult as strands of algae became entangled in the propellers. Campers and picnickers no longer fancied drinking the water. Cottagers wanting to pipe water from the Lake found the filters of their water pipes became blocked with green slime.

Algae are plants. They need sunlight in order to live. When the layer of algae on the Lake became too thick, the algae at the

32

bottom of the layer could not get any sunlight. They died and sank to the bottom. As the dead algae decayed, they used up oxygen. This meant that there was not enough oxygen available for fish, and the fish died. This was a big disappointment to the many keen fishermen in Canada. The Lake became so bad that there were only eels and sludgeworms left.

What can be done to bring back life to a 'dead' lake?

One answer is to bubble oxygen through it.

British Oxygen's river protection service

It is too costly for a lake the size of Lake Erie. It is done on small stretches of polluted water in the United Kingdom. The photograph above shows the use of oxygen to fight water pollution. A method which has been used in a smaller lake in Sweden is to pump out some of the dead and decaying matter.

These methods are very expensive, too expensive to use on a huge lake like Lake Erie. So what action did the Canadians take? They felt they could not stop the farmers using fertilisers. Instead they decided to tackle the effluent coming from Cleveland, a big industrial city on the American side of the Lake. The Americans agreed to cooperate because they too were disgusted with the state of Lake Erie. They were also in a mood to agree because of an almost unbelievable event that happened in Cleveland. The river that flows into Lake Erie caught fire! This is not an exact statement of what had happened. What really caught fire was methane gas. Methane is formed when sewage decays in water which is short of oxygen. A layer of methane on top of the water caught fire, and a bridge across the river was burned. This shocked the citizens of Cleveland, and they decided to clean up the river. As a result, the deterioration of Lake Erie has been reversed. It is now showing signs of recovery, although the fertiliser problem remains.

33

SOAP OR DETERGENT: WHICH IS BETTER?

Should we use soaps or detergents? Detergents pollute the water; soaps do not. Soaps and detergents are chemically similar. It is the substances called 'builders' which are added to detergents which cause the trouble. They are phosphates. They have two jobs to do. One is to make the water alkaline, which makes removal of grease easier. The other is to combine with calcium ions and magnesium ions which are present in hard water. Detergents are very powerful cleaning agents. They have the big advantage that they work in hard water.

Soaps do not work in hard water. The calcium and magnesium ions in hard water form a scum with soap. If a water-softener is used, to take out the calcium and magnesium ions, then soap will give a lather. Instead of using detergents, we could use soap and a water-softener.

People certainly seem to prefer the cleaning action of detergents to soaps. In 1948, detergents had 10 per cent of the cleaning market, and soaps had 90 per cent. In 1953, detergents had 50 per cent of the market. Now, the figure is 80 per cent.

There is another difficulty about abandoning detergents and going back to soap. Soap is made from vegetable oils and animal fats. The food industries also want to use vegetable oils and animal fats. Detergents are made from crude petroleum oil. The petrochemicals industry makes all kinds of things from crude oil. It makes better sense to make detergents from crude oil, and use fats and oils for food.

Perhaps you would like to try some of the experiments on the cleaning power of detergents in Activity 10.

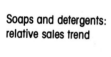

Soaps and detergents: relative sales trend

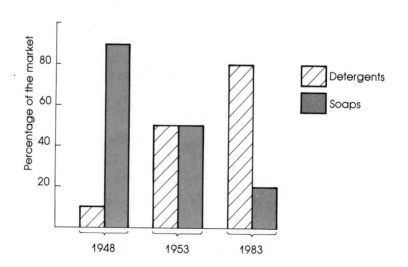

34

Construct a model water-softener

The diagram below shows one way of making a model water-softener. It uses a substance called Permutit®, which is used in domestic water-softeners. Water must be run into the top of the tube slowly. With the screw clip open, water will trickle slowly out of the tube into the beaker.

You can test the water to see how soft it is compared with the tap water.

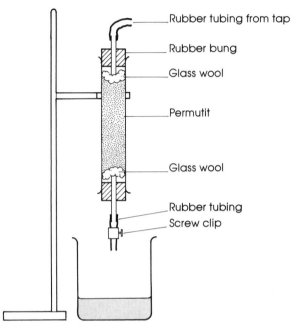

A model water-softener

Rubber tubing from tap

Rubber bung

Glass wool

Permutit

Glass wool

Rubber tubing

Screw clip

The next diagram shows an experiment to find out how many drops of soap solution are needed to give a lather. You measure 25 cm^3 of water. Then, you add soap solution 5 drops at a time. You must count the drops as you do so. After each 5 drops, you stopper the flask and shake it. You will see flakes of scum

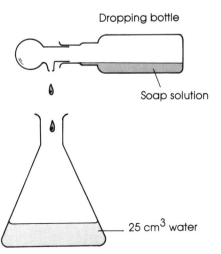

Dropping bottle

Soap solution

Adding soap solution

25 cm^3 water

forming on top of the water. This is not lather. Lather has a frothy appearance. When a lather is formed and lasts for 30 seconds, stop adding soap solution. You have now added enough to get rid of all the hardness. Write down the number of drops of soap solution used.

It is interesting to compare results from:
>   Tap water
>   Boiled tap water
>   Tap water + a crystal of washing soda (sodium carbonate crystals)
>   Distilled water
>   Water from a model water-softener.

Which method gives the softest water? Is this the method you would recommend for domestic use? If not, why not? (See page 54.)

(See page 54.)

ACTIVITY 9

Make a bar of soap

Many books give directions for soap-making.

ACTIVITY 10

Experiments on soaps and detergents

For these experiments you need:

>   Soap solution
>   Packets of: soap flakes (e.g. Lux®), non-soap detergent (e.g. Persil®), a detergent which contains soap (e.g. Fairy Soap® or Fairy Snow®), an enzyme detergent (e.g. Biotex®)
>   Cotton rags and a selection of staining materials, e.g. tea, coffee, orange juice, blood, egg, grass, sump oil, cooking oil
>   Aluminium foil
>   Magnesium sulphate
>   Oven
>   Powdered charcoal
>   Universal indicator
>   Top-loading balance
>   Liquid detergent
>   Sodium nitrate
>   Calcium phosphate.

EXPERIMENT 1
Which disperses dirt better—soap or detergent?
Step 1   Put a tiny amount of powdered charcoal with $100 \, cm^3$ of water in a conical flask. Stopper the flask, and shake well. Does the powder disperse (spread out) through the water?

Step 2 Repeat with water to which you have added one of the following:

  (1) 2 cm³ soap solution
  (2) 2 cm³ non-soap detergent
  (3) 2 cm³ of a detergent which contains soap.

Compare your results with page 54.

EXPERIMENT 2

Which is better at making oil mix with water—soap or detergent?

Step 1 Half fill three test-tubes with water. Into each put 1 cm³ of oil from a teat pipette.

  To (1), add 2 cm³ of soap solution.
  To (2), add 2 cm³ of detergent solution.
  To (3), add nothing (this is the control).

Step 2 Cork each tube, shake vigorously, and allow to settle. Look at the three test-tubes. Which has emulsified the oil (made it mix with water) better—soap or detergent?

Compare your results with page 54.

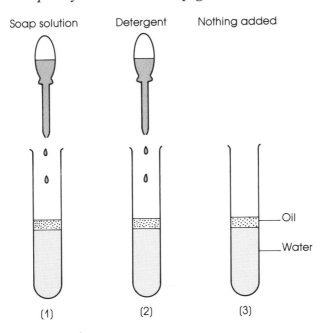

Oil and water

Soap solution   Detergent   Nothing added

Oil

Water

(1)   (2)   (3)

EXPERIMENT 3

Do soap and detergent lather in hard water?
Step 1   Number four test-tubes. Place them in a rack. Half fil
them with water. To test-tubes (2) and (4), add 0.5 g of magnesium sulphate crystals. Shake until all the crystals dissolve.

Step 2   To test-tubes (1) and (2), add 1 cm³ of soap solution.
To test-tubes (3) and (4), add 1 drop of liquid detergent. Shake
all the tubes. Observe which test-tubes have a lather. Does any
tube have a result other than lather? Does magnesium sulphate
allow soap to lather? Does it allow detergent to lather?

Compare your results with page 54.

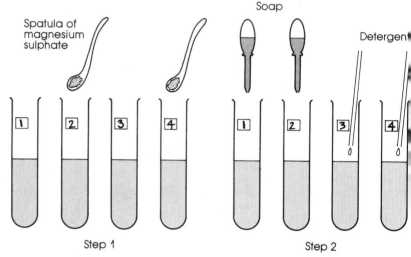

EXPERIMENT 4

Which are the most alkaline detergents?
Step 1   Make up solutions (1 g in 1 litre) of the detergents
you have collected. Label the solutions.

Step 2   Take one solution in a test-tube. Add 5 drops of
universal indicator. Shake the test-tube. Compare the colour
with the universal indicator chart. Write down the pH number
Solutions with a pH greater than 7 are alkaline. The higher the
pH, the more alkaline the solution.

Compare your results with page 54.

Matching against the
the colour chart

EXPERIMENT 5

Which are better—enzyme detergents or non-enzyme detergents?

Note. An enzyme is a large protein molecule with a very special job to do. Its job is to assist a chemical reaction which takes place in a plant or animal. It might be one of the reactions which takes place when we digest our food. The enzyme speeds up the reaction.

Step 1 Take some squares of cotton rag. Stain them with different substances. You might try egg, orange juice, tea, grass, coffee and many others. Leave the stains to dry.

Step 2 Prepare 1 per cent solutions of an enzyme detergent (e.g. Biotex®) and a non-enzyme detergent.

Step 3 Label a set of beakers:
  Egg + enzyme detergent
  Egg + non-enzyme detergent
and so on.

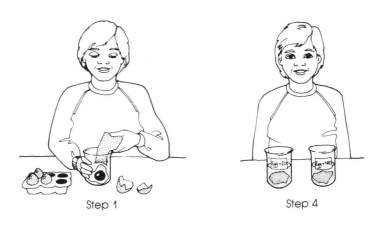

Step 1   Step 4

Step 4 Cut each square of cloth in two. Put half the egg-stained cloth into the beaker labelled 'Egg + enzyme detergent' and the other half into the beaker labelled 'Egg + non-enzyme detergent'. Add the correct detergent to the two beakers.

Deal with the other pieces of stained cloth in the same way.

Step 5 After 30 minutes, fish out the pieces of cloth. Which are cleaner—the ones soaked in enzyme detergent or the others? (See page 54.)

Extension Work You can extend this experiment. You found out in Experiment 4 which detergents are strongly alkaline and which are weakly alkaline. You could compare their cleaning power by the method you used in Experiment 5. You might try different detergents and different stains.

You could design an experiment to test whether the detergents work better in cold water or hot water. Again, test different stains.

You could compare the ease of washing out fresh stains and dried-on stains. Do detergents work better if the stain is fresh?

EXPERIMENT 6

Which detergent gives you the most for your money?
Note. You can see that the prices of detergents vary. It is interesting to find out whether they all contain the same amount of water. You can then compare the price with the water content. This will help you to decide which is the best buy.

Step 1 Make a small flat-bottomed tray from aluminium foil. Tear off a 10 cm square of aluminium foil. Pinch the corners together, as in the diagram. Fold the corners along the sides of the square to make a tray. Press the corners together so that the tray will hold liquid detergent.

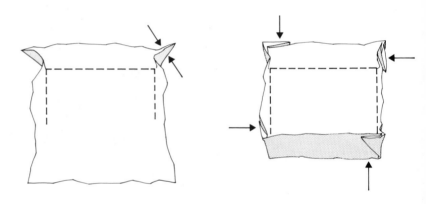

Step 2 Weigh the tray on a top-loading balance. Write down the weight. Weight $= w_1$ grams. Put about 5 g of detergent into the tray. Reweigh. Weight $= w_2$ grams.

Step 3 Put the tray into an oven at 110 °C. Leave it to dry for an hour or overnight. Reweigh the tray. Weight $= w_3$ grams.

Step 4 Calculate the percentage of water in the sample:
Weight of sample $= w_2 - w_1$ grams
Weight of water $= w_2 - w_3$ grams

$$\text{Percentage of water} = \frac{w_2 - w_3}{w_2 - w_1} \times 100\%$$

Work out the price of each detergent per 100 g. For example, a bottle containing 500 g for 31p costs $\frac{31}{5} = 6.2$p per 100 g.

Step 5 Repeat the test with other detergents. Make a table of your results. Which detergent has the lowest price? Which has the lowest water content? Can you spot a 'Best Buy' which gives the most detergent for the money?

Table of Results

Detergent	Price in p per 100g	Percentage of Water
Whizz	6.2	20

EXPERIMENT 7

What makes algae grow?

Step 1 Obtain some pond water with algae floating in it.

Step 2 Half fill seven beakers with the pond water. Add to each of the beakers one of the following, labelling each beaker as you do so:

    (1) 1 g detergent
    (2) 10 g detergent
    (3) 1 g sodium nitrate
    (4) 10 g sodium nitrate
    (5) 1 g calcium phosphate
    (6) 10 g calcium phosphate
    (7) Add nothing.

Step 3 Stand the beakers in a light place. After 2 weeks, some beakers will show a thick growth of algae.

Extension Work Can you think out a way of weighing the amount of algae formed in each beaker?

QUESTIONS ON SOAPS AND DETERGENTS

Supply words to fill the spaces in these passages. Do not write on this page.

1 Soaps and detergents remove ____ and ____ from cloth. Both soap and detergent ions have long chains of ____ groups. These form a 'tail' which is water- ____. Soap ions and detergent ions also have a 'head' which is water- ____. When clothes are washed, the heads of soap ions are attracted to ____, and the tails are attracted to ____. Thus, soap ions form a bridge between ____ and ____. This helps ____ to float off the cloth into the water. Dirty water must be removed by ____. In hard water, ____ work better than ____.

2 Soap is made from oils and fats by boiling with ____. In soft water, soap produces ____. In hard water, ____ is formed. The reason is that ions of the metals ____ and ____ are present in hard water. They combine with soap to form ____. If you go on adding soap to hard water, in the end, ____ is formed.

3 What is removed when water is softened? What crystals can be added to water to soften it? (Give the trade name and the chemical name.) What water-softener is put into columns so that water can trickle through it? Which method of softening gives the purest water? Why is this method not employed for use in the home?

4 What are algae? What is the connection between detergents and algae? Describe what happens to swimmers and boaters when algae multiply. Why is this more likely to happen in a lake than in a river?
Algae cannot go on multiplying indefinitely because they exhaust their supply of a certain substance. What is it? What happens when algae run short of this substance? Is any plant or animal other than algae affected?

CROSSWORD ON SOAPS AND DETERGENTS

First, trace this grid on to a piece of paper (or photocopy this page). Then fill in the answers. Do not write on this page.

Across

1 In ____ water, it is difficult 19 across, 14 down (4)
3 It must have been seen over the river in Cleveland (5)
7, 15 across Add this to soften water (7, 4)
10 See 20 across
11 A useful thing to do the washing in (7)
13 Chemical symbol for aluminium (2)
15 See 7 across
16 A new washing powder will need a ____ before it is sold to the public (5)
17 Short for saint (2)
18 Produced by soap in hard water (4)
19 (2 words), 14 down This is why you add soap (2, 3, 6)
20, 10 across This is what you must give clothes after washing with soap or detergent (8, 5)

Down

2 A way of getting very pure water (12)
4 Salts of this metal make water hard (9)
5 This substance is used in domestic water-softeners (8)
6 An old-fashioned way of warming the water is to put it on this (4)
8 Chemical symbol for nickel (2)
9 The parts of soap ions which are water-loving (5)
12 Grease helps dirt to ____ to fabrics (5)
14 See 19 across
18 You can use a ____ for adding soap powder (5)

43

THE BOUNDLESS SEA

A drop in the ocean

The seas are so vast that we have assumed that they will absorb all the rubbish we dump in them. In recent years, there have been more and more accidents involving oil spillage at sea. The sea has not been able to cope with it all. Accidents at oil rigs in the sea and at oil terminals, where tankers load and unload, may discharge oil into the sea. Some oil tankers flush out their oil tanks at sea. This is illegal: they should do this in dock while delivering their oil. To do it at sea saves time, but it is a dreadful act of vandalism as it pollutes a vast area of sea.

Some of the oil evaporates, some dissolves, but most of it floats on the surface of the sea. Slowly, air oxidises it to carbon dioxide and water. Slowly, bacteria decompose it. But oil remains for a long time, and can do a lot of damage.

There was an accident involving an oil tanker called the *Amoco Cadiz* off the coast of France in 1978. Miles and miles of the beautiful beaches of Brittany were spoiled by thick oil washing in from the sea. Brittany is normally a very popular holiday area, but people gave it a miss that year. It lost money from the tourist trade. The fishermen had a bad year too as their catches were low.

The first time the United Kingdom had to deal with a huge oil slick was in 1967. The oil tanker *Torrey Canyon* sank out at sea, off the coast of Cornwall. Eighty million litres of oil started flowing towards the coast. Detergent was sprayed on to the oil slick in huge amounts. Unfortunately, this proved not to be the best way of dealing with the problem. The oil slick spread further over the surface and affected even more seabirds and fish. The detergent proved poisonous to many creatures too. People refer to it as 'the *Torrey Canyon* disaster'. Thousands of seabirds were killed.

What can be done?

First, what can be done to prevent oil spillage at sea? France has 'spotter' planes, which fly over the English Channel and

The Torrey Canyon

watch out for cargo ships discharging oil into the sea. They take photographs of any ship breaking the law. France also has fast boats patrolling the Channel. They can make contact with any ship which is causing contamination. Some captains, sailing far from their own countries, are not as worried as they should be about polluting the sea. If they know there is a chance of their being spotted by a plane or boat, they are less likely to break regulations. A fine is imposed on any company whose ships break international law.

Oil from the Torrey Canyon on a Cornish beach

Five million litres of oil pass through the Channel each day, yet the United Kingdom has no spotter planes or patrol boats. Should we keep a closer watch on the Channel?

An Esso tanker

Secondly, what can be done about accidental spillage of oil at sea? A good example was set by San Francisco in 1971. Two tankers collided in thick fog under the Golden Gate Bridge. Three million litres of oil spilled into San Francisco Bay. Fortunately, after the oil had flowed 4 miles into the Bay, the tide turned, and the oil ebbed out. But when the tide turned again, it brought the oil flooding back along the Pacific coastline. It trapped tens of thousands of birds which winter on the shores of San Francisco Bay.

The Standard Oil Corporation accepted responsibility for dealing with the damage their tankers had caused. They did not rush in with detergent, because the *Torrey Canyon* disaster in 1967 had shown that this was not the best remedy. They rushed 40 000 bails of straw to the coast, which may seem a strange way to deal with oil. The straw was dropped into the sea by helicopter, from barges and boats, and pushed into the sea by volunteers working on the shore. Straw is able to soak up from 5 to 40 times its own weight of oil. When soaked with oil, the straw had to be picked up again from the sea. Some of it was picked up by cranes floated out in barges. Some was picked up by people going out in boats with pitchforks—2000 pitchforks went into use. Thousands of volunteers stood on the beaches, picking up the bales of sodden straw as they washed

A cormorant covered
with oil from the
Torrey Canyon

ashore. The straw was loaded on to trucks and driven away to
be dumped in pits. For three days, volunteers and oil company
employees worked around the clock to protect the coastline.
The map shows how the oil spread and where fouling of the
beaches occurred.

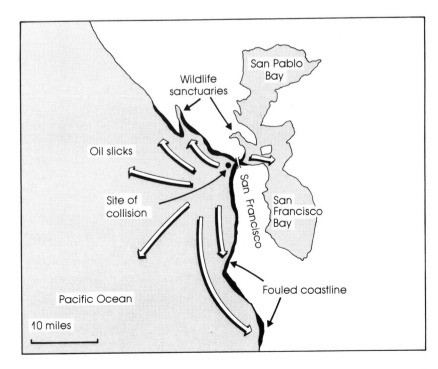

San Francisco Bay

San Pablo
Bay

Wildlife
sanctuaries

Oil slicks

Site of
collision

San Francisco

San
Francisco
Bay

Fouled coastline

Pacific Ocean

10 miles

Standard Oil spent £2 million on cleaning up. They sucked up a large amount of oil from the sea with vacuum pumps. Tanker lorries were driven on to barges, and floated out to sea. Pumps sucked oil from the sea into the tanks. Then the lorries were driven to refineries where the oil was reclaimed.

Another technique was to make floating barriers. Volunteers made a floating barrier to keep the oil from entering Bolinas Lagoon, a sanctuary for seabirds.

A clever idea was to make a line of floating booms. One end was attached to a barge, and the other to a small boat. The boat set off from the barge and made a circle round bales of sodden straw. Then it headed for the barge, towing the bales of straw with it as shown in the diagram below. The crew of the barge pitchforked the sodden straw aboard.

What happened to the birds? Seabirds sit on the sea and dive for food. These poor birds dived into clean water and came up into thick oil. The oil matted their feathers, and they could not fly. Many drowned. Their insulation from the cold water was ruined. They were tossed helplessly to and fro on the water, and many died before they reached the shore. Those that were still alive were wrapped up and taken to cleaning stations.

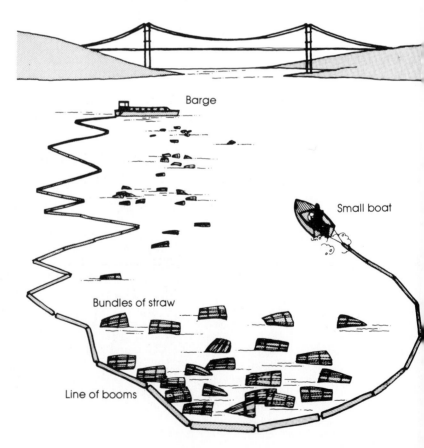

Barge

Small boat

Picking up sodden
bales of straw

Bundles of straw

Line of booms

Standard Oil supplied 100 000 litres of mineral oil to clean them. Volunteers bathed the birds in mineral oil and dried them in flour. They were then cared for until they could swim again. The oil company paid out £500 a day for food and medicines. In spite of all this care, only a very small fraction of the birds survived. You may be interested in Activity 11, which is about removing oil from feathers.

This story shows how ordinary people can play a major part in fighting pollution. All kinds of people thronged to the beaches to pitch in. They worked all night in January weather. What kept them going was the feeling that in fighting for their environment, they were fighting for themselves. The detailed experiences of the San Francisco oil spill have been written down so that the techniques they learned can be used to help other people in the future.

Chemists too have been hard at work, looking for a way to attack oil spills. At the British Petroleum Company, they have discovered chemicals that have the most amazing effect on oil. When sprayed on to a film of oil, they turn it slowly into a dry, rubbery solid. Chunks of the solid can be collected in nets. If any of the solidified oil escapes the nets and washes ashore, it can be peeled off the beach like a rubber sheet. The chemicals have been tried out in the laboratory and also in experiments at sea. One day, they may prove their worth in fighting pollution.

ACTIVITY 11

Ways of cleaning oil-soaked feathers

Step 1 Look at the way feathers repel water. Drop water on to a feather from a teat pipette. See how the water runs off the surface.

Step 2 Smear sump oil on six feathers.

Step 3 Put a 1 per cent solution of soap flakes into a boiling tube. Put one of the feathers into the boiling tube. Leave it for

5 minutes. Move it gently around from time to time. After 5 minutes, take it out, and leave it to dry.

With the other feathers, try other cleaning agents, e.g. solutions of detergents, and solvents such as propanone and ethanol. *These are flammable liquids. Take care.* You must NOT have a lighted Bunsen or any other flame around.

Step 4   When the feathers are dry, look at them carefully. Make a note of which looks the cleanest. Now test the feathers you have cleaned to see how they repel water. Which treatment has the worst effect on the feathers' ability to repel water?

Extension Work   You can try rubbing feathers with cleaning agents and solvents, instead of soaking them. You can try taking off the oil with an absorbent material such as sawdust.

QUESTIONS ON POLLUTION

1   The word *pollution* has been used many times in this book. Explain what is meant by pollution of water. What are the most common causes of pollution in rivers? What are the most common causes of pollution in lakes? Is it possible to pollute the sea?

2   The word *conservation* is used to mean keeping our environment clean and healthy. Explain what needs to be done to keep rivers and lakes clean.

3   List all the recreational uses for rivers and lakes that you can think of. Do any of these uses pollute the water?

CROSSWORD ON WATER POLLUTION

First, trace this grid on to a piece of paper (or photocopy this page). Then fill in the answers. Do not write on this page.

Across

1 France uses _____ planes to look for pollution (7)
5 Where 2 down may be spilt (3)
6 When spilt, 2 down can spread over a large _____ (4)
7 The UK had to pay a huge _____ when 3 down 13 across broke up (4)
8 Apparatus for getting oil from under 5 across (3)
10 The Irish Republic—anagram of 16 down (4)
11 Many birds have been _____ by 2 down pollution (6)
13 See 3 down
14 Its crew gathered polluted straw (5)
17 If it is polluted, fish may die (5)
19 This is how you could describe the San Francisco beaches in 1971 (4)
20 It transports 2 down (6)

Down

1 A spillage of 2 down (5)
2 A fuel that floats on water (3)
3, 13 across This 20 across sank in 1967 (6, 6)
4 Great anger (4)
5 All sea captains should put this first (6)
9 The 1 across planes fly over the _____ (7)
12 A bird may get this polluted with 2 down (3)
13 _____ up the countryside by removing rubbish! (5)
14 France has more than one fast one patrolling the 9 down (4)
15 Water falling and carrying pollution? (4)
16 This lake was once very polluted (4)
18 This caused the collision in San Francisco Bay (3)

A FINAL WORD: POLLUTION AND CONSERVATION

What is water?

Water is a compound of hydrogen and oxygen. It has the formula H_2O. It is a very good solvent for many substances.

What is pure water?

Pure water is water which contains no dissolved substances. It is very difficult to obtain pure water as it is such a good solvent for many substances. It tends to dissolve a little of any substance with which it comes into contact. Distillation can be used to give pure water.

What is polluted water?

We call water 'polluted' when it contains substances which are harmful to life. A polluted river has less plant life and fewer fish than a clean river. The main sources of pollution are:
1) People's body waste—sewage
2) Industrial waste
3) Insecticides and fertilisers.

Why do we need to protect water from pollution?

Diseases are spread by dirty water. Polluted water is a danger to health.

Polluted water is likely to become unpleasant and smelly. People like to use rivers and lakes for recreation. They cannot enjoy themselves in polluted water.

River-water is taken to the water-treatment works and made fit to drink. If the river-water is polluted, the treatment is much more costly. It may even become impossible to make the water fit to drink.

What is conservation?

The word conservation means keeping things the same. People talk about *conservation of the environment*. By *environment*, they mean the world about us—the air, the water and the land. By *conservation* of the environment, they mean keeping the air, water and the land in the same clean and healthy state it was in before our society became so industrialised. People who are very interested in conservation are called *conservationists*. Conservationists are not opposed to progress. They do not want to do without the benefits of modern industry. What they do want is for us to keep a sharp lookout for the side-effects of industry. Some of these side-effects are polluting the air, the water and the land. Conservationists want us to make sure that our lives do not become poorer because we have let our environment become unhealthy and unclean.

Have you ever thought about doing your bit towards conservation? You may not be in a position to do what the people of San Francisco did, but there is plenty you can do. You could get a group together and go round with sacks, picking up litter. You will be surprised how much you enjoy it if there is a group of you working together. You could reclaim a spoiled area. Some girls we know saw an area near their school that was an eyesore. They weeded it, sowed some grass seed and planted some shrubs and flowers. Now it is a very eye-catching corner. It gives them satisfaction to see it on their way to school, and know that it is all due to them. Some boys and girls we know worked on the banks of a canal. They weeded, and removed dead wood and litter. They uncovered a footpath which had become overgrown. People can now walk along the canal. It is now a pleasant area for recreation. The group who did the conservation work enjoy it more than anyone.

HOW DO YOUR RESULTS COMPARE WITH OURS?

Activity 1

1) (a) about 1 litre or 2 pints (b) 4 to 9 litres or 1 to 2 gallons (c) varies, about 4 to 9 litres, 1 to 2 gallons (d) 4? litres or 10 gallons (e) 4 to 9 litres or 1 to 2 gallons.
2) (a) 5 litres or 1.1 gallons (b) 50 litres or 10 gallons (c) 1? litres or 3.3 gallons (d) 50 litres or 10 gallons (3) 15 litre or 3.3 gallons (f) 15 litres or 3.3 gallons.

Activity 8

Distillation gives the softest water. It is too expensive for use i? the home. Permutit® gives the next best result, and is suitable for use in the home. Washing soda is cheap and is a good water-softener.

Activity 10

Experiment 1 1) Powder is not dispersed at all. 2a) Powder disperses at first, but soon sinks to the bottom or rises with scum. 2b) A good permanent dispersion. 2c) The result depends on the relative amounts of soap and detergent in the brand used.
Experiment 2 The layer of oil is thinner in the test-tube 2) with detergent added. Detergent makes oil mix with water: detergents are emulsifying agents.
Experiment 3 1), 3) and 4) lather; 2) has scum. Detergent lathers in hard water but soap does not.
Experiment 4 Examples are Stergene® pH 7 to 8, Lux® flakes 10 to 11, washing-machine detergent 10 to 11, washing up liquids 7 to 8.
Experiment 5 Enzyme detergent works better, especially on food stains.